ORANGE FRAGMENTS TO READ AND
CONTEMPLATE IN A SUNNY DAY

PHILOSOPHY SERIES: 1

Orange Fragments to Read and Contemplate in a Sunny Day

By Çetin Balanuye

Copyright © 2022 Transnational Press London

All rights reserved. This book or any portion thereof may not be reproduced or used in any manner whatsoever without the express written permission of the publisher except for the use of brief quotations in a book review or scholarly journal.

First published in 2022 by Transnational Press London in the United Kingdom, 13 Stamford Place, Sale, M33 3BT, UK.
www.tplondon.com

Transnational Press London® and the logo and its affiliated brands are registered trademarks.

Requests for permission to reproduce material from this work should be sent to: sales@tplondon.com

Paperback
ISBN: 978-1-80135-154-6
Digital
ISBN: 978-1-80135-155-3

Cover Design: Nihal Yazgan
Cover Photo by Scott Webb on unsplash.com

Transnational Press London Ltd. is a company registered in England and Wales No. 8771684.

ORANGE FRAGMENTS

TO READ AND CONTEMPLATE IN A SUNNY DAY

Çetin Balanuye

TRANSNATIONAL PRESS LONDON

2022

CONTENT

About Author 2
A BITE TO REPLACE THE PROLOGUE 3
CHAPTER I: REALITY 5
CHAPTER II: ENCOUNTERS 37
CHAPTER III: CONTEXT 117

ABOUT AUTHOR

Balanuye is a Turkish continental European philosopher and academic. His book *Where Does Spinoza's Joy Come From?* [published in Turkish only] went through numerous editions and contributed to the adoption of Spinoza's teaching by outside readers as well as philosophers in Turkey. He currently teaches at the Department of Philosophy at Akdeniz University.

A BITE TO REPLACE THE PROLOGUE

Philosophers are generally expected to engage in the three pursuits together and meticulously for a sufficient amount of time: reading, thinking, and arguing *for* or *against* by writing or speaking.

According to this approach, it is possible for everyone to practice a philosophical life. Because the said approach does not allow an "all or nothing" type of rigidity; some may be more involved in this pursuit, some less. In any case, there is a difference of degree rather than a difference of type.

It should be kept in mind that in the definition put forward, reading, thinking and discussion are nonetheless necessary but not sufficient elements to be an original philosopher. Allocating a serious place to all three elements in her life does not guarantee an original philosopher. Authenticity is a gem we still don't know enough about.

The book in your hand consists of fragments, the shortest of which is a sentence and the longest of which is a few paragraphs. I wanted these fragments to invoke longer readings, reflection practices, and perhaps discussions, triggered by shorter readings.

Almost all of the trailers focus on various facts; ordinary everyday facts gleaned from books, newspapers, or encyclopedias. I tried to turn each fact into a creative trailer experiment with as few words as possible. This experiment undoubtedly had great predecessors: Heraclitus and Aurelius from the distant past, Pascal more closely, Nietzsche, Adorno, Canetti, and today Galeano or David Shields are just a few of these names. I feel like a mischievous kid sneaking into these masters' labs; I'm desperate, I can't do anything else, I'm very curious about what's going on in the experimental environment.

I hope you forgive me.

CHAPTER I: REALITY

Time

The "time" we talk about and the "time" that hurts us are not one and the same thing.

This is another way of expressing the fact that philosophy will always endure.

Ecstasy

The only superiority of reality over ecstasy is the brazen permanence of the former.

Ontology

The 'a' in the expression 'a wind blows' whispers that man is destined to always see individual beings around him, whose boundaries are supposedly obvious.

Life

The sun is rising. Plankton and plants will still live today. The rays of light will be sugary again, without even moving a blade of the green cover... and the turtle that has set out from the night will bite the first leaf of the day.

Hopefully, to eat sweet and talk sweet.

Lie

A lie works, but it is not valuable.

If there were no such thing as truth, lie would even be valuable. In 2015, two scammers managed to sell a fake Goya painting for 1.5 million Euros.

The lie had worked, except that the scammers later realized that the money paid to them was also fake.

Philosophy

There have always been two paths before philosophy: to understand human beings and/or to understand the conditions that make human beings possible.

Contrary to popular belief, the second way is humbler.

Ethics

Diarrhea is the second most common cause of death in children younger than 5 years of age and its treatment is to make the child drink plenty of water.

Even this simple fact is difficult to reach in societies dominated by superstition. There will always be someone who says, "Angels give water to a child with diarrhea." If you say, "Angels give water to a child with diarrhea," death will occur. If you say, "Give the child with diarrhea plenty of water", life will last.

According to Spinoza, "ethics" is the work of living by striving to increase adequate knowledge of the second kind.

Qualia

Knowing our insignificant place in a vast cosmos is useless when a tiny nerve in the dentist's chair is being manipulated.

This is a mocking reality!

Absurd but authentic.

Poem to Gallium*

You're tough, don't I know?

So much to melt in my palm.

[* Gallium: A type of metal. It melts slowly in the warmth of the palm, gaining its former hardness away from the heat source. It could be argued that some people have a Gallium spirit.]

Entanglement

Objects and ideas are entangled with each other.

After the Sudoku puzzle came out, sales of pencils increased by 700%.

An idea is born, turns into ink spots on paper; people, wood, coal, paint, shipping, accounting move to interact with it.

Individuation

98 percent of the atoms that make up our body are renewed every year. None of us are the atoms of last year. Despite this repetition, we remain "the same" to the extent that our DNA is successful in replicating itself.

But provided that you understand the "same" here correctly.

This is a sameness that is possible only with repetition, as Deleuze says: It is *repetition with difference*.

Truth

Saying that truth is possible is different from saying that one has attained knowledge of the truth.

While the former brings man closer to the virtue of authenticity, the latter can turn him into a universal tyrant.

In the first, there is the sincerity of an everlasting search, and in the second, the arrogance of a snob or of a despot.

Magic

35% of our world is made up of iron. We owe our discovery of the magnet to this abundance of iron.

According to ancient Greek and Chinese sources, people always thought the magnet was magic.

We will continue to mistake things for magic, according to Arthur C. Clarke: "Any sufficiently advanced technology is indistinguishable from magic."

Starry cinema

If we do not count the short-legged, stubby-beaked, ugly migratory birds that come by once a year, ours is the village where no one is seen except the unfortunate people who fit in these 70 houses.

But... We have one passion in common: to watch the skies at night. Together with the crowd, merrily, laughing dreamily.

[The common passion of the residents of the small village called "Saadat Shahr" in the Iranian countryside was to observe the sky. They even built an observation tower by uniting and saving money. At night, everyone would turn off the lights and meet at the tower.]

Saturn's rings

The cute 12-year-old girl said to her father: "Even if dinosaurs had telescopes, they wouldn't be able to see Saturn's rings."

Father said pedantically: "Of course, how will an animal see?"

The girl contemptuously corrected: "Ugh, that's not the point! Those rings didn't exist when dinosaurs went extinct."

Perception threshold

The world we see when we turn our heads is full of various objects. What we call an "object" is understood by a single criterion: Our threshold of perception!

I felt a faint ache in my neck just as sleep had nearly taken over my consciousness. The smallest tangible needle tip had taken a reluctant step into the skin of my neck, and that momentary tension between the needle and the surface of my skin had paid off in the needle's favour.

These small, perhaps the smallest flies are called Phelobotomus. They are so small that it is as difficult to distinguish them as to distinguish "nothingness". They have two wings. Transparent. Noticing a flying Phelobotomus is like touching a dream.

My eyes, which are willing to sleep, roll to the side helplessly. You can't look at your neck. The painting on the wall is an original riot of stains. A good example of modern painting, whose figure is redrawn each time according to the beholder. My eyes freeze at the painting at the tired and indecisive insistence of my consciousness. The flutter marks of the brush created roughness on the surface. The elevations and cavities are stained with the manners of the colors – like countless dots. When I generalize my gaze, the stain turns into a figure; when I focus my attention, the figure disappears. I don't know why I keep on playing this game I've gotten myself into.

My neck is aching. I'm not ready to scratch. Where is Phelobotomus? I discern a wiggle in the stain of the painting. I read that a good picture keeps drawing itself. Could the dots be alive? Leibniz's monads come to mind, which have their own purposes, which cannot be divided or changed, but which come together and create new beings. The moving point remained. I am ready to doubt my perception. Well, the eye tingles… Just then the flicker repeated. Phelobotomus was put on the painting!

With this awareness, I thought about what separates the painting from Phelobotomus. What distinguished Phelobotomus from the spots, dots, and lines in the painting? What could this game of detecting, which I can change with the attentional distance I provide in my gaze, teach me about the difference between Phelobotomus and painting? What would Phelobotomus look like if I had the opportunity to take a closer look? Moreover, would the practical comfort that I gave him by calling him Phelobotomus continue? Or would the singularity of Phelobotomus remain? I thought it was just one of the specks that made up the stains on the painting earlier. Can't I just be thinking that it's a Phelobotomus now?

Could speaking of the singular be the result of absolutizing a human perception scale?

Closure

The idea that life should have a meaningful closure is an adult obsession.

Childhood is the last objection to this.

In the story written by a 5-year-old girl, meaning defies totalitarian uniformity: "Once upon a time there was a forest. Lots of animals and they weren't very good. The little girl was very scared. Then a crocodile appeared. The end."

Reality

Our inner world may be very rich, but man takes place on the outside.

What was it David Shields was saying? "How can I tell what I think until I see what I say?"

Telos

The saying "Life has a way of knowing" is mostly true; however, it is not possible to conclude from this that "whatever life throws at you is part of a grand cosmic plan".

Life is neither crazy nor wise.

It resists reconciliation with the meaningful closure we call 'knowing'.

Walking

The first experience of confidence in the body is walking.

The ground knows no tricks.

Yet sometimes we stumble. Far from casting doubt on this friendship, stumbling gives our feet a humble opportunity for self-criticism and insight

Galileo

New Scientist magazine, published since 1956, announced in its November 7, 1992, issue:

The Catholic Church, which pressured Galileo to renounce his theory that the earth revolves around the sun, confessed 359 years later:

Galileo was right.

Unbearable

Our ears are made of wax, shaped at the mercy of our desires.

This is why we can hear lies so easily when we are deaf to the truth.

Other than Philosophy

His interest in philosophy turned into a passion at a young age.

For this reason, he studied physics, chemistry, biology, botany, and geology incessantly, and whenever he had time, he also read the basic works of philosophers.

Conatus

Some ideas have an almost natural determination to survive. Not only those who adopt it, but also those who openly object, continue to reinforce it; because that idea has made it impossible to think in the old way that preceded it.

Evolution is such an idea.

Human

Human thinks that she alone can choose in the universe.

It is not just a superstition; it is also useless.

This belief has not been seen to prevent any great evil. Still, the monument to animals lost in the war in London reads: "They didn't have a choice!

Virtue

Oh man! You did not understand us.

In fact, man is always a premature birth. To put it simply, we are literally premature beings. Our large brain diameters do not pass through any mother's birth canal, so we are the ones whose brains will grow outside.

This is why we are obliged to a virtuous environment.

Diamond

The hardest and most durable thing known, diamond is "adamas" in ancient Greek.

It means "unchangeable or never broken". In reality it both changes and decays, but this takes billions of years. However, a human lives 110 years at the most. It's an awareness that's hard to face. She finds the cure in denial.

A human's passion for the diamond is a confession of an expensive denial.

Drunkenness

If someone says, "drunkenness is essential for the right decision," it would be read like an empty statement trying to get attention.

However, Herodotus said that the Ancient Persians would think twice about any idea: once when sober and once when drunk.

A good idea retained its charm in both cases.

CHAPTER II: ENCOUNTERS

Meeting

"The number of people I felt happy not to meet in this society exceeded the number of people I was happy to meet," she said.

She was either too prejudiced or too far-sighted.

I cannot see her anymore.

Sapere

As we understand from his letters, Darwin not only studied many of the animals he discovered, but also ate them.

Is it simply a curiosity for new flavors? It doesn't look like that. Darwin seems to be aware of the connection between "knowing" and "swallowing and digesting" what is good for you.

Etymology comes in handy here: "Sapere" in Latin has two meanings: the first is "to know wisely", the other is "to taste".

Destined to be a writer

One of the giants of Italian literature, Giorgio Manganelli warns those who plan to seek to be a "good writer" around literary chairs: Are you saying you are Shakespeare? It is possible; moreover, I believe in it. That's why I say: Sign up for geology. You will see how many metaphors will be gifted to you.

Manganelli's critique as cool as a paper cut reveals that an inspiration from stones sails through language rather than drowning in the terms of literary theory. There are many masters who can be supposed to have heeded this suggestion; for example, Herman Melville: In which literature department would you find the wealth of imagination provided by the long years on board?

There will be those who would object, recalling someone who lived away from objects in a pattern of everyday life woven only from words: Jorge Luis Borges encountered neither fossils nor granite in the dim corridors of his library; there will be those who will say that this did not prevent him from becoming a great writer.

Certainly, but it would be an understatement to think that Manganelli simply asked what business we were dealing with and was more concerned only with that. Metaphors, images, and fictions can be so fluid that they seep through the walls of a library. But what will draw them in is the author's colorful interest, believing that in every creation of the cosmos, large and small, there is a mystery that deserves a close scrutiny. Only such an interest could bring the madeleine chocolate together with Proust, a white horse with Cortasar, or the scent with Suskind.

Exaggerating theoretical interest and under-estimating environmental awareness may have more serious consequences than preventing the birth of genius. Polanyi bluntly explains that if we take each of our steps with obsessive attention, we will disrupt the spontaneous flow of walking, and we will stumble.

Literature turns into a magical revel as language feeds on environmental interest; the quality of this harmony is largely the result of the cosmos's flirtation with language.

Child

I watch the children with shoes that light up as they walk. It is their turn to live. They will grow. They will never pay so much attention to their steps again.

The lights of the shoes will go out. Feet will turn into docile followers.

They will walk the paths of adults.

Squirrels

Squirrels store seeds for the winter and then forget where they are.

Many millions of trees are the work of this fleeting forgetfulness.

Upbringing

The child shapes the world like plastic.

It becomes an adult when it turns into plastic formed by the world.

Man

The phrase 'love is blind' may be more than a metaphor, at least for men.

Male ladybugs would realize something was wrong after more than four hours of courting a long-dead female.

I wish

The old midwife, who was responsible for naming, grabbed the baby by the feet and looked at his face for a long time.

His temper was already evident. An ascetic was born who would always favour the past against the future.

She named it "I wish".

Souls

In ancient Greece, people did not eat beans.

Because they believed the souls of the dead were trapped in beans.

Beans have a great place in the modern cuisine. For we thought of drinking mineral water after swallowing the souls.

Virtuous

Renowned cellist Yo Yo Ma left his three-century-old Stradivarius cello, worth $3.5 million, in a New York taxi.

There were only minutes left before the start of her magnificent concert when the tension finally ended.

It was considered fair by everyone that the taxi driver watched the concert for free at the forefront with the protocol.

The Devil

In 2005, a young Catholic girl in Romania died at the hands of a priest, crucified as part of an exorcism ceremony, and starved for days with her mouth shut.

It is not known if there was a demon, but a priest was definitely there.

Encounters

Sometimes people say, "I read, but nothing remains".

I think this is an unfounded complaint.

According to the findings of brain plasticity studies, which are now creating a large and exciting collection, every encounter or experience of any kind, big or small, whether we are aware of it or not, creates new neural pathways in our brain.

If they told me to name an encounter that is effective even when forgotten, I would say "a well-written book".

Stealing

Stealing someone else's idea without realizing it is called "kleptomnesia".

An 'innocent thief' with all sorts of brilliant ideas can suddenly turn up out of any of us.

How are you?

Knowing that people have already agreed to leave each other in deadly solitude, we take the same risk repeatedly every day:

How are you?

Fortunately, no one makes us regret our mettle by acting with unnecessary sincerity

.

Thought experiment

One day in the future, an academy of philosophy called "If My Grandma Had a Beard" will be established.

Here, the answer to this question will be sought: "What would be possible with man under completely different conditions?"

Our contemporary philosopher, George Lakoff, exemplifies one of these: "What would our number system be like if man were not a biped but a reptile?" He also shares his guess on the answer:

The number system we use, and our concepts of addition and subtraction are the result of our evolution as bipedal animals. Mathematics would be very different from what it is now, if we were not animals that travel distances with discontinuous strides.

Cat

Of all the things to learn from a cat, 'playing with your own tail' is the most important.

The tail is a furry symbol of mastery of time with yourself.

... and what you can never learn from a cat is 'self-pity'.

Lonely tree

The loneliest tree on earth was that tenere tree: the captain of a solitary life in the middle of the Sahara Desert, 400 km from the nearest tree.

It was not far enough from the human species, however.

One night in 1973 – it is not known how – a driver's car crashed into it and overturned.

Patriotism

It is the same idea as an astronaut planting an American flag on the Moon and shooting migratory birds on the grounds that they are foreign agents who come to mess with his country every year around the same time.

People think their fictions are real.

[The American flag on the Moon is now whiter than white due to radiation from the Sun.]

Twins

In the Nazi Concentration Camp, Joseph Mengele's scientific research was mostly aimed at twins.

As soon as one of the twins died, the other was also killed; so, Mengele could perform a comparative autopsy.

At Auschwitz, the twins shared not only their appearances but also their destinies.

Dreamfish

The "Salema Porgy" fish when eaten produces hallucinatory effects.

When this feature was discovered in Ancient Rome, people made it a habit to leave their minds to the mercy of this fish in special entertainments.

The 'dreaming fish' had been turning into a creative artist in the dreams of the person who digests her.

Superiority complex

Crows are said to be extremely intelligent; they can drive, recognize similarities; their memory is also strong.

But arrogance is unique to us.

We say, "crows are as smart as a 7-year-old", but we cannot say "as smart as a crow" even for a 3-year-old child.

Male

One study found that 77% of women are "sapiosexual".

In other words, they found the intelligence of a man sexually most arousing, rather than any other feature.

The result of the research made all men happy without exception.

Woman

In the 4th century B.C. Athens, a skilled physician was ordered to undress before a distinguished jury of the judiciary.

As the male-dressed physician slowly undressed, a thin-boned female body began to grit the masculine teeth of justice.

Agnodice's unpardonable crime was to study medicine even though she was a woman.

Noise

A Yanomami woman who has always managed to distinguish between self-confidence and arrogance at first sight was asked how she managed to do this.

The old woman spoke in her own language with various signs. She said something like this:

"The first is in a tree by a river or on a hill, and is silent; in man it is arrogance, it makes noise.

Don Juan

The passion for self-expression is the hidden motive behind the desire to meet new people.

It disguises itself as flirting among the sexes; We beg the other as if to say, "Listen to my story and appreciate it."

Someone once said of the notorious womanizer Don Juan: "For him, a woman is just a virgin ear."

Orgasm

"The devil's laugh!"

This was Arthur Schopenhauer's name for the serene post-orgasmic awareness.

It was the moment when the woman realized that she was part of a universe that did not care about her happiness... a moment when she realized she was a slave to her biology.

Becoming

We find a flawless design in every structure —natural or linguistic – in which we are born without witnessing the process of its formation, and we look for its designer.

In Nicaragua, 50 deaf children were placed in the same school in 1970, who knew no sign language, and they developed a unique language in 10 years.

Today this language is called "Nicaraguan Sign Language".

Weakness

If your arms are tied behind your back, your anger should be directed at the one who binds your arms, not against those with free arms.

The expression of resentment in the weak is the opposite.

Poverty

My father used to think the hand-knitted market net bag was the perfect invention.

He also learned to knit a net bag. To him, the net bag's only flaw was its inability to hide its contents. He would feel embarrassed: there were those who could afford it, and those others who could not!

He especially remembered this fault when he managed to bring home a bunch of bananas*.

[* In the 70s, bananas were an expensive fruit for middle and lower class families in Turkey.]

Partisan

Rade Končar, one of the symbols of the resistance against fascists in Croatia, has a statue called 'partisan'.

Someone who tried to pull down the statue fell under it and was seriously injured.

The dogmatism of the aggressive subject against the prescient object. Like a masterpiece image.

Aging

The senses weaken as we age; perhaps this is why our mind's vision develops gradually.

Of course, this is not the rule: some not only silently witness their senses atrophy as they get older, but also realize with gloomy sincerity that they do not have the sharpening of the mind to make up for this loss.

Carnivorous

In 2014, Chinese elite guests were waiting in the restaurant to taste the famous chef's legendary "cobra soup".

Chief Peng Fan's cry of pain was heard. The cobra, which he left to cook with his body in the cauldron but his head out, had bitten him.

That evening there were two bodies in the kitchen and nothing to eat

Power

It is called "Lion". A dog. A resident of a garden near the sea in Adrasan. With an immense body and a large heart. Big-bodied, brazier-hearted.

An aggressive guest dog challenged him. It hurt, but he wouldn't get into a fight. Finally, he could not take it anymore. He raised one enormous paw and smashed his opponent's head to the ground with tremendous force.

After locking the culprit for a while, he softly licked it and released it.

Arrogance

The human species believes that the entire universe is preoccupied with it.

In the 80s, some underwater sounds recorded by the Swedish navy became the cause of a diplomatic crisis with Russia.

Magnus Wahlberg was awarded the Nobel Prize for parody for revealing that the sounds come from fish farting.

Totalitarianism

The phrase "smoking is harmful to your health" can be far more lethal than cigarettes, depending on who is saying it.

Latin

Veni, vidi, flevi.

I came, I saw, I cried.

The Other

You can put a child to bed and watch until she falls asleep.

Adults cannot sleep with eyes fixed on them.

The "other" has now become a threat.

Types of suicide

Trees cannot run away when people try to uproot them.

Even if they tried, we would have caught them.

Because humans are suicidal animals

Cowardice

The difference between "being alive" and "living" becomes clear when you're in a vegetative state, connected to a machine.

Also, in cowardice.

Studies say that cowards have a better chance of surviving. Forgetting to add that as long as they stop living.

Being up to date

I was meeting with a 94-year-old relative of mine for the first time in a long time, who I thought had been smoking since the day he was weaned.

I noticed that he no longer smoked. "What happened to the cigarette?" I asked him curiously. "I quit," he said.

He also explained the reason: "I heard that it is harmful to health."

Self-deception

Interestingly, there is no "self-deceiving animal" among the common definitions of humans. However, of all animals, only man is capable of deceiving himself at every opportunity.

"Hey! The cheeky dancing fire, you won't be able to take what I love!"

His scream suggests a hero who is trying to save his family from the fire. Not a man in front of his barbecue trying to get his cutlet off the embers.

No risk!

On long bus journeys from one city to another, when the bus stops, I read sadness and loneliness on the faces of people who get off the bus and move about to satisfy their needs.

I always wonder why.

I have concluded that the space-time between "arriving at" and "leaving" a place creates anxiety in people.

Is being in-between a foreign feeling to man? Maybe.

Or perhaps man is a weak being who finds peace only in safe repetition.

Love of dad

The top of my father's neck was my favourite sitting place in our 69 model single-door blue Anadol.

I used to count the vehicles that my father passed and that passed him on the short trips we made as a family to the surrounding provinces, trips that were affordable in our limited budget.

When I always had him come out on top, my father asked: What's up?

I didn't tell him I even counted parked cars, too.

[* Anadol is a domestic and cheap automobile of Turkey, which was produced for the last time in the 70s.]

Body

Tournier advises the photographer in his essay "Naked Portrait": If you are going to shoot even a portrait, ask your model to undress completely. An aura emanating from the naked body will add a unique authenticity to the face.

Spinoza used to say that we don't know what a body is capable of.

Economic security

For many, a small pension means the freedom to spend time on their own.

According to Theodore Zeldin, this was not so innocent either.

Prussian landlords invented the pension in the 19th century as a bribe to keep workers away from a socialist revolution.

Desire

Desire... The majestic zoomer that fends off all threats.

In the movie, from the dialogue between the woman who slept with her best friend's husband and the other woman:

- Weren't you ashamed when you did this to me?

- The feeling of shame is unfortunately not strong enough to suppress the desire.

Georges Bataille also said: Desire seeps out of all the cathedral ruins.

Poetry

The first false relationship with poetry begins with reading poetry aloud to the crowd.

Thus, the poem closes itself.

Unless the mouth is closed, it will not open again.

Praise

The cat from Adrasan* showed me the bird that was chirping around it: "I am the one who resists all these provocations, but you people say that the tortoise is peaceful, and I am the predator. Is there anyone who provokes the tortoise so much? Has he ever managed to stay cool despite being so aroused? "

"God gives everyone as much load as they can carry, you shouldn't whine for a mere trifle," I said, and added:

"Hunt, if you can!".

[* Adrasan is a Mediterranean town in southern Turkey, famous for its brilliant sunlight, sea and forests.]

Love

The affection whose object has not yet settled in the memory is called love.

Becoming other

It is said that "man is what he eats".

Perhaps it can also be said: Man is what he defeats.

After Alexander defeated the Persians, he began to dress like them and chose two Persian women as wives.

You must be careful about who you beat.

Healthy death

Capitalism first destroys all the nutritional value in the potato and then makes us believe that the healthiest cooking tool for the potato is "steam".

It never forgets to add that health is important.

Thus, while children grow up "healthy", their parents who can't afford the expenses die of cancer.

Education

Education is like watering a flower; it must be impossible to tell who gave the water by looking at the leaves.

Leisure

The English word "school" derives from the Ancient Greek "skhole", meaning leisure.

Leisure in the modern era is what is left of school.

Hunger

Superstition quickly loses its power in the face of a hungry body.

According to common belief in the British navy, you should not whistle at sea, as it will arouse strong winds.

Even while cruising, only the cook can and *should* whistle: to make sure he doesn't eat while he's doing his job.

No way

Those who feed mainly on "memory" and those who feed on "senses" can be understood at a glance: the first group is sensitive but wistful, the second is callous but cheerful.

We are those who could neither be in the past nor in the present: we tumble between remembering and perceiving.

Elitism

Historically, in England, milk was put into the cup first, then tea, because cheap porcelain cracked when it first met the heat.

Increasingly, putting the tea first became a sign of prosperity and elitism.

This is how capitalism is: it gives glory to the weak in itself, from everything outside of itself.

Conscience

Conscience did not descend from the sky; it is the eyes and voice of the society we inhabit.

He sees you – in spite of you – and talks to you.

If it is quiet, the society outside has long since fallen into decay.

Shower

The excessive extravagance in the days of peace is the cause of all wars.

Capitalism sets up the game with the command to save in war and waste in peace.

There are two types of shower concepts in the USA: the navy shower and the Hollywood shower.

The first flows intermittently and tells you "water on, wet down, lather up, water on, wash down "; the second flows continuously and uninterruptedly at the desired temperature.

Habit

In fact, David Hume was the first to sense this: The 'morally right action' is to exhibit the automatic reflex of picking up the potatoes that have fallen out of the bag of someone walking in front of you – without any mental assessment.

It is habits, not reason, that activate the moral muscle.

Confession

It was illegal to be an atheist in the Nazi army.

Soldiers had to register Protestant, Catholic, or at least "believe in God."

Hitler already understood that the only way to cooperate with humans for sustainable evil was for them to have faith so that one day they would be forgiven.

Doors and cats

The cat's anger at the door is conditional: If it is closed it does not like it.

Maybe cats cannot tolerate closed doors because they want to be where they are not.

While some people are like cats, others cannot do without a door that separates them from the outside world.

Poetry

Sincerity may be necessary for good poetry, but it is not sufficient.

The poet's emotional undressing guarantees a naked poem, not good poetry.

As Oscar Wilde said: All bad poetry is sincere.

Creative memories

"Remembering" is rather "creating the memory".

It is like a piece of chocolate or jelly, not a marble you put in your pocket yesterday. When you take it out, it takes on a completely different form.

Literature discovered the tricks of memory very early on; neurology now confirms it.

Schizophrenia

I came, I saw, I went mad.

[According to a study published in the journal *Frontiers in Psychology*, schizophrenia is not found in congenitally blind people.]

Witch

In the winter of 1780, a 40-year-old woman became a maid in the house of a distinguished physician in Switzerland.

She was fired when nails came out of the children's bread and milk. Later, when one of the children fell ill, she was accused of witchcraft. She was executed by beheading in 1782. The last "witch" in Europe was Anna Göldi.

The Swiss court considered the case again in 2008, and Göldi was finally acquitted.

Our distinguished physician, Johann Jakob Tschudi, actually had sexual intercourse with his maid.

The woman was the victim of "an elite and masculine slander."

Twins

Tatiana and Krista, the Canadian conjoined little twin girls, never looked into each other's eyes.

But since their "thalamus" is conjoined, one can perceive the feelings and ideas of the other – and is triggered by them.

This is a drama that will not allow any hypocrisy between them.

Notice me

Finding twelve stones stacked on top of each other in a remote nook of a deserted forest shows that another person was there before you, and also one who could not help but show that he was there.

Arrogance cannot tolerate not to be noticed.

Alchemy

A puppy was left in the garden of an orphanage.

The work of striking alchemy: Hundreds of broken-hearted little hands turn the pain in the dog into playful barks with a pat on the head.

Promotion

The only way to be raised to a higher position in some jobs is when your employer has a big criminal file that nobody knows but you.

Bosses never leave loyalty to chance.

Loneliness

"The loneliness of a matryoshka doll is so unbearable that you can't even imagine it," said, the youngest child of a large family.

Resistance

The biggest mistake of our civilization is to think that saying "please, after you" is more civilized than "I will risk everything to protect my bread and butter".

As you like it!

Human relationship is more often than not a duel rather than a duet.

It is up to you.

It is either "good to be like that" or "unfortunately like that".

Inheritance

The extraordinary 17th-century artist Ninon de l'Enclos was a woman who resisted marriage and childbearing in order to preserve her independence.

She was making quite a bit of money. When she died, it was understood that she left her money to her accountant's 9-year-old son, who was keen on books.

The boy's name was Voltaire.

Fallibility

Let one see that his basic beliefs are simply wrong. If this happens at an early age, he will either foolishly rebel or bend his neck with a bitter but honest wisdom.

Once he's old enough, he settles only for the first option.

Sourdough

There is no necessary relationship between aging and maturation.

Some are simply old people and their unpolished nature is as bright as the first day.

Poetic

Louis Jenkins, the great master of the genre also called "prose poetry," has recently died.

In one of the small bites he wrote: "The Aztecs thought that for the sun to rise every morning, they had to sacrifice a large number of people. And it worked! The sun came up every morning."

Anthropocene

There is a city in Brazil called "Nao-Me-Toque"; it means "don't touch me!".

I have always considered it unfortunate that it should have been the name of our earth, instead of a mere city.

CHAPTER III: CONTEXT

Context

Context matters. If the words "Love takes a lifetime, making love a minute" were written in a Kinsey Institute* brochure, the effect would be traumatic.

[*Kinsey Institute: A research institute established in 1947, famous for its research programs on human sexuality and relationships.]

Philosopher

It is impossible for a philosopher to misunderstand a question; The problem - on the contrary - is that the philosopher always gets the question right.

This is why his answer is so rarely understood.

Lonely buddies

The fault of language is not that it provides incomplete communication, but that it provides perfect communication.

After all, we had the entire universe in front of us as a group of cosmic loners who only understood each other.

Meaning

The space between the two words is a confession; admits how loose-permeable the skin of a word is.

Meaning comes in flow, oozing from one word to the next.

A perfectly self sustained word has not yet been created that does not leak meaning to another word by keeping its meaning to itself.

Thank gods!

Advice

An education guru is popping up all over the place and constantly telling young people to "dream and follow your dreams".

Young people, on the other hand, continue to stand with a deadly stillness as they hear this. All of them are terribly aware that this bullshit speaks to only "one" lucky person out of 100,000 people.

Are there any education gurus who give another type of advice to young people?

"Not only you young people, but all of us should have revolutionary dreams! There is no salvation alone. Either all together or none of us!"

Rigor

You cannot pick up a nail and write haphazardly on a stone; that's what the paper came for.

We reached the pinnacle of carelessness with the keyboard.

Progress continues.

Self-confidence

Is the diagnosis of "lack of self-confidence" or "high self-confidence transformed into humility" appropriate for someone who is most surprised when he achieves something?

It is one of the grandiose stories about narcissism: When Caesar was kidnapped by pirates, he asked asked them for the ransom to be increased.

Caesar must have felt that his value was not well recognized. However, many people feel like Caesar about it. We do not limit our generosity when we give ourselves points for how valuable we are.

There may be some among us who truly deserve this rating. Admittedly, the personal achievements of some people may not be recorded in history. The problem is that everyone considers himself one of these people. Yet, our personal judgment of what we are worth is often useless; the capacity of others to be influenced by us has the final word. It is a world where it is not what we are but how we are perceived that matters.

Walt Disney was fired from his job at a newspaper in Missouri at the age of 22. He was told he was not "creative enough" as the reason for his dismissal

Language

It is weird.

Man is born mute, speaks quickly, and is then enslaved by language.

The Object of Desire

The object of desire.

It's always at the top of the sold-out list.

Mind

The human mind has a multi-layered structure.

In stories, fairy tales, and even in everyday life, although we often express that something happens first, then something else, and then another, in fact, many things happen at once and our minds distinguish these things with different clarity. While we are eating, we notice the sounds coming from outside as much as we are interested in our food; stimuli from the television at that time trigger some thoughts; our memory constantly occupies our minds. Our mind keeps working like a collection of parallel layers placed on top of each other.

Despite this astonishing performance of the human mind, it also has a weakness that most of us are not aware of: In the various overlapping bustle of everyday life, if we do not show special effort and discipline, our mind turns into an insignificant tape recorder. Then these different impressions go through a process, and we give the certain simple reactions to these various experiences.

However, the human mind does not consist of such a small number of functions as seen in many other living things. Only a human being can, at least from time to time, get rid of the routines of daily life and turn to that privileged function we call "thinking". He pauses to react impulsively to random stimuli of the environment, becomes quiet, focuses, and thinks; sometimes of a question, sometimes of a detail.

Thinkers assign different values to this human predisposition. For example, Heidegger says that this kind of "reflective focusing" is not as decisive as it is thought in the general practice of being; on the contrary, life mostly continues more like in a habitual fashion. For Ortega, this predisposition is indispensable: there is no creativity without being drawn in!

Proust's mind is remarkable as regards this discussion: in the *Swann's Way*, the narrator experiences the smells and sounds emanating from the environment and the ideas leaking from his memory in the present and in the same original order. He focuses while telling, but continues to live while focusing.

The Proust's novel is neither merely an attempt at introspection nor straight description. Rather, it is an aesthetic illustration of the possible activity potential of the human mind.

Elegance

There are about 20 "lone deaths" a year in Amsterdam; homeless, without identity and without ceremony.

A poet - Frank Starik - derived a personal responsibility from this sad situation.

Now, whenever there was a solitary death in the city, there was a flowery burial and a poem addressed to the dead.

Reading

What is taught in primary school is not "reading" but "straight reading".

Schools and teachers must be highly skilled in this business, as almost everyone has become a straight reader, and can read the waybill receipt or postal address.

"Reading", on the other hand, is a demanding, strenuous and advanced skill that resists straight reading.

Religious

Different religions have different beliefs.

Since all of these cannot be true at the same time, the following two options remain: Either all but one or all of them are false.

This picture does not cause the religious people to doubt because each of them necessarily thinks that luck is on his/her side.

I love you

The development of a sense of "I" in humans is also the beginning of tragedy.

Feeling oneself as an indivisible whole means an effort to preserve that unity at all costs. You get tired of the being you protect while you keep protecting it; your inability to stop protecting makes you cheeky.

One can abandon the arrogance of an 'I' only for the temptation of being another 'I'! Love is an effort to find another "I" that will rewrite, redraw, dissolve, but also reconstruct me.

Fear of disintegration is the first cause of the feeling of love.

Thou shall not steal!

Among the books stolen from libraries in The United States, the classics written on ethics stand out.

Stealing a book that says stealing is wrong is perhaps the 'final crime'.

Or a thief is a skeptic who says 'I will not stop stealing before I read'.

Or he is a thief who wants to emphasize the irrevocable fact: "I steal, therefore I am."

Justice

The concept of 'justice' is different from and broader in scope than the concept of 'law'.

For some, however, the most glorious is 'conscience'.

James Buchanan, the 15th president of the USA, did not approve of slavery, but he knew it was legal. He found the solution by buying slaves and freeing them with his own money.

Appreciation

Famous writer Maupassant says that he finds the Eiffel Tower ugly, moreover, he ate his meals at the restaurant on the ground of the tower, since it was the only place where he would not see this freak.

It is not enough to be brave to express our appreciation sincerely; it is necessary to have deserved this courage.

Paid work

"Free slavery" is not an oxymoron.

In the feudal period, the free man did not work; mandatory labor was the fate of the slave.

Today mandatory labor is the condition of so-called freedom.

We all have been made to believe that we will be freed as a slave to a job where you can never get your labour's worth.

Causality

Instead of questioning what good education should look like, asking how much it will cost is the cause of a country's poverty, not the effect.

Stranger

It is a deeply rooted disposition for man to seek evil in what is unlike himself; this is why we cannot find societies freed from this predisposition, although it is possible to find individuals.

In the Roman Empire, an institution similar to today's The Foreign Office was fittingly called the "Barbarian Bureau".

History of ideas

Someone who was deceived by everyone he met insisted that "I was never fooled".

They called him "romantic" and the narrator of this story "realistic".

This is how romantic realism was born.

Neo-liberalism

The cheater wants more people who condone cheating, but is afraid that everyone will cheat.

Neo-liberalism is a "deception partnership".

It calculates the ideal equation that shows how many people can join the partnership at most.

Luxury

Being stylish is not the same as dressing expensively.

The first is more transparent and shows you. The second, on the other hand, is a thicker veiling and makes something very important invisible even in the most *décolleté* form: modesty.

Patriotism

For some, the idea of war and the love of the nation is one and the same thing, they think that they are in debt to their country if they do not die while fighting for it.

Czech general Zizka – a person of this kind – found a way to die in peacetime.

After he died, a drum was made from his skin – a drum to be played in battle.

Childhood

The calendar of memory knows no equality. Childhood lasts long.

However, everyone's experience of their own childhood is different. For some, childhood is an inexhaustible rich hat from which the magician draws all kinds of surprises; for others, it is a dim cellar where a few unpleasant memories remain silently.

Experience resembles a gum. Everyone stretches their childhood. Depending on the consistency of your gum, it either gets longer as you pull it, or it shrinks and breaks in the first pull.

Reproach

People reproach each other almost every day: "Why don't you ever call me?"

Behind all such reproaches lies the reproachful person's naivety to find herself interesting.

Queen

Being the wife of a king can only fuel romantic dreams of queenhood as long as things go well at home.

When the king of Thailand brought his first wife to court to divorce, the woman did not even have a chance to defend herself.

The laws forbade any criticism of the monarchy.

Nobility

One of the two words can be 'elite' and the other 'cheap', although the concept they refer to is almost common.

'Bank robbery' and 'theft' are examples of this.

According to the US law, in order for the crime to be recorded as the first type, the act has to be committed during working hours.

Authenticity

'Solitude' and 'loneliness' are two different concepts.

The first is a well-deserved gift, the second is a deserved punishment.

Sense of justice

Some people have a strong sense of justice, or of injustice as the case may be: They didn't choose, it happened to them.

While they are burning with the passion of 'truth', they become one of two things: wise or crazy.

Which they become depends in part on themselves, in large part on the society of which they are a part.

Capitalism

It was W.M. Wheeler who had first observed: Sometimes ants would misinterpret the tracks, forming a circular convoy that would plunge the entire colony into disaster. The march of this dysfunctional caravan almost always ended in death. This was called the "ants' death vortex".

Capitalism is the name of a similar vortex.

Familiarity

A popular science book should be useful "enough".

It can be downright harmful if it is too useful.

Too much familiarity flirts with lack of understanding.

Nationalists

A bill was proposed for inclusion in the US Constitution in 1916: Every declaration of war by the government would be put to a national popular vote, and those who voted 'yes' would be deemed to have accepted and committed to military service.

The bill was not accepted.

Eros

Eros. The Greek God of love. Increases desire, love and coupling with the arrow he shoots.

Really, what happened to Eros?

[In the USA, a weapon was invented for the police to use to catch a suspect with a rope thrown from afar.]

Conscience

Everyone is guilty to one degree or another, but guilt is not felt equally.

A feeling of guilt that one will laugh at may be the reason for another's life-long suicide.

Not only income, but also conscience is unequally distributed.

Law

The judge was always asking the same question to the witness, who knew both the plaintiff and the defendant very closely: Did the defendant call the plaintiff "dishonorable"?

The witness was silent. The judge repeated the question, but got no answer.

Finally, the witness spoke: "Your Honor, you keep asking, did he always say 'dishonest?' When are you going to ask, 'is he dishonest?'"

Duet or Duel

When people are young, they want their relationship with the opposite sex to be a duel, but as they get older, they settle for duets.

Insight

A person's ignorance is revealed the first time he accuses the world of injustice.

Paternalism

Every society makes some inventions to make life easier; for example, fever reducers work regardless of religion, language, race or gender.

Malaysia, on the other hand, is the land of inventions that only make men's lives easier:

A man who texts his wife "I divorced you" three times on his mobile phone in one SMS is officially divorced.

Longing

If we were asked, is it difficult to endure torture or to control our desires, we would probably say the first.

This is doubtful.

Some of the victims who survived the Holocaust died from excessive consumption of chocolate and confectionery in the early days of their liberation.

Naivety

The majority of those who continue to believe in other people despite being deceived in the past.

An extreme fear of trusting people as a result of such an experience is called "pistanthrophobia".

This phobia – interestingly – is rare, so cheaters have no trouble finding new victims.

Memory

He was the god of remembrance

I wished him a butterfly life

Every moment is full of laughter.

["Hyperthymesia" is a neurological disorder characterized by a complete recollection of past experiences. Derived from the ancient Greek words "hyper" (excessive) and "thymesis" (remembering).]

Aging justice

Justice is only manifested in movies.

This is because of a 1.5-hour summary of, say, 50 years of life full of inconsistencies.

Time is cunning and patient. Life obsoletes justice, corrupts revenge, makes heroes look like everyone else by wrinkling their faces.

Know yourself!

The carpenter's apprentice masters the wood as he or she suffers; the jigsaw, which in the beginning was makeshift in his hand, begins to dance, the chisel begins to fly, and the grater begins to twinkle.

Conversely, an apprenticeship in philosophy begins with a high level of self-confidence: A philosopher is a master whose voice becomes hoarse as he gets older and his speech loses its fluency.

Innocence

The kindest person in the world was an inventor.

Rumor has it that he devoted his life to one goal: to develop glasses that would show the babyhood of the person being looked at. He believed that this would stop all evil.

When he learned that there were also those who harm babies, he stopped and became invisible.

Man and marriage

The biggest unhappiness of a married man is having a happy marriage.

There is not a single valid reason to disappear.

Loyalty

"Loyalty" is, ironically, a virtue that can only be expected from a seducer.

Why should we praise those who find themselves innately prone to monogamy for the mere reason that they are faithful to their mates?

No one appreciates a frog for being able to jump in water.

www.ingramcontent.com/pod-product-compliance
Lightning Source LLC
Chambersburg PA
CBHW071700170426
43195CB00039B/2393